ELEMENTS

poems by

JAMES

GALVIN

Copper Canyon Press / Port Townsend

The magazines in which some of these poems appeared are: *APR,*
Atlantic, Field, Quarterly West, Sonora Review, Partisan Review,
Missouri Review, Iowa Review, and *Crazyhorse.*

The author thanks the National Endowment for the Arts
for a grant that helped.

The publication of this book was supported by a grant
from the National Endowment for the Arts.
Copper Canyon Press is in residence with Centrum at
Fort Worden State Park.

The Sabon type was set by Fjord Press.
The symbols on the book are Chemical Signs
from Rudolf Koch's *Book of Signs.*
Book design by Tree Swenson.

COPPER CANYON PRESS
P.O. Box 271, Port Townsend, Washington 98368

Contents

ELEMENTS

The Heart

A stumblebum in scree.

A hummingbird with internal bleeding.

A desert windmill churning out
Its painful water,
Gurgling *like, like, like.*

This must be the pursuit of happiness,
Which is no one's right.

A game the heart plays hurting.

A butterfly with sore feet.

The windowstunned bird willing
To batter itself further
For its birthright the air.

Someone reciting an original poem
With his throat cut.

Testimony

You can't step into the same
River even once,
And why would you want to? You can't
Lie down without turning your back
On someone. The sun slips
Like butter in a pan.

The eastern sky arrives
On the back stoop in its dark
Suit. It draws itself up
Full height to present its double
Rainbow like an armful of flowers.
Thank you, they're lovely.

I step outside where the wind
Lifts my hair and it's just
Beginning to rain in the sun,
And the earth silvers like a river
We're in, I swear to God,
And you can't step out of a river

Either. Not once.

Against the Rest of the Year

The meadow's a dream I'm working to wake to.
The real river flows under the river.
The real river flows
Over the river.
Three fishermen in yellow slickers
Stitch in and out of the willows
And sometimes stand for a long time, facing the water,
Thinking they are not moving.

*

Thoughts akimbo
Or watching the West slip through our hopes for it,
We're here with hay down,
Starting the baler, and a thunderhead
Stands forward to the east like a grail of milk.

*

The sky is cut out for accepting prayers.
Believe me, it takes them all.
Like empty barrels afloat in the trough of a swell
The stupid bales wait in the field.
The wind scatters a handful of yellow leaves
With the same sowing motion it uses for snow.

*

After this we won't be haying anymore.
Lyle is going to concentrate on dying for a while
And then he is going to die.
The tall native grasses will come ripe for cutting
And go uncut, go yellow and buckle under snow
As they did before for thousands of years.
Of objects, the stove will be the coldest in the house.
The kitchen table will be there with its chairs,
Sugar bowl, and half-read library book.
The air will be still from no one breathing.

*

The green of the meadow, the green willows,
The green pines, the green roof, the water
Clear as air where it unfurls over the beaver dam
Like it isn't moving.

*

In the huge secrecy of the leaning barn
We pile the bodies of millions of grasses,
Where it's dark as a church
And the air is the haydust that was a hundred years.
The tin roof's a marimba band and the afternoon goes dark.
Hay hooks clink into a bucket and nest.
Someone lifts his boot to the running board and rests.
Someone lights a cigarette.
Someone dangles his legs off the back of the flatbed
And holds, between his knees, his hands,
As if they weighed fifty pounds.
Forever comes to mind, and peaks where the snow stays.

Sociology

A small white
Envelope appeared under the door
And it was the beginning of the world.

No one opened it
Which brings us to the present.

A fly hits the windowscreen
Like a distant pistol shot.

We fall asleep

And the story being read us
Keeps going,

About an otherwise young man
Who turns suddenly white

While buying an orange on the street.

Paradise of ashes, fragrant nights,
The sun doesn't know what time it is
Or up from down.

Don't cry,

In the story it is nice out
And they eat some soup.
Under the door

A small white envelope appears
And they open it.

The Story of the End of the Story

To keep from ending
The story does everything it can,
Careful not to overvalue
Perfection or undervalue
Perfect chance,
As I am careful not to do in telling.
By now a lot has happened:
Bridges under the water,
No time outs,
Sinewy voices from under the earth
Braiding and going straight up
In a faint line.
I modify to simplify,
Complicate to clarify.
If you want to know your faults, marry.
If you want to know your virtues, die.
Then the heroine,
Who resembles you in certain particulars,
Precipitates the suicide
Of the author, wretchedly obscure,
Of that slim but turgid volume,
By letting slip:
Real events don't have endings,
Only the stories about them do.

Genesis

Not in wilderness to beguile them
But in a garden, which is wilderness beguiled.
Not in reason but in temptation,
Not in compassion but in judgement.
Not for better and not for worse.
Not for an idea.
Not for the atom that cracks, the flower that opens,
Not for the newspaper bursting into flame,
The ultimate nail, driven in. Not for love,
Not on their lives,
Whose relative happiness or virtue
It was not for,
Not for, not for, not for.

Coming into His Shop from a Bright Afternoon

Like a local flurry or stars too small to use that spilled, iron
filings stain the dirt floor silver.
                                   In the center of the floor,
the forge, in the center of the forge, the rose the bellows angers.

He lights a cigarette on rose colored steel then hammers the
steel over the anvil's snout.
                              Red sprays of sparks splash from
each strike.
             One gummy, fly-speckled window begins to allow a
sprawl of wrenches, brushes, punches, chisels, taps, gauges . . .

Coalsmell.
          Sweat.
                 The distant blue his eyes are.
                                               There is a lathe
and milling machine, both homemade from scraps.
                                               He chooses a
lighter hammer.
               Now I can read the names on varnish cans and see
how the walls are layered under sawblades, snowshoes, an
airplane propeller, a loom.
                           On the other side of the door at my back, the

light I came in from grows white like a blizzard or hot steel.

Hammer blows ring across the meadow too much like bells.
                                                    He is
shaping a piece of earth.
                        He is hammering it into what he wants.
He thrusts it back into the fire when it loses its blush.

Regard

In regard to their own movement
The stars we track have no inkling.
They're just burning.
Is the willow less in winter?
God's a far cry and busy
Counting dead ants, dead stars.
In regard to its own movement the willow tree
Knows less and less.
Now and then now and then
I forget what I am saying
To myself, often
When you touch me,
Even if we are just wandering down this street
On the surface of a planet
Turning through the fire.

Cartography

Out on the border a howl goes up, skinning the cold air.
A windrush as if from enormous wings descending
Slicks the grass down and thumps, and the whole sky bruises.
Out on the border it stops just as suddenly
As if there were some mistake, and there is: mortal beauty
This world can't bear, and a skeletal silence
Administrates the clouds, their passages, their dissolutions
                                                    in light.

Out on the border right and wrong are more distinct,
But the border itself is suggestive, permissive, a thinly dotted line.
Amassed armies of forests and grasses poise,
Encroach, but never cross.
Even the sky stays on one side.
Another howl goes up, not a threat as was thought,
But an invitation to an interior. The border

Halves a piece of paper into here and hereafter.
A man, himself a fascicle of borders, draws a map and can't
                                                    stop drawing
For fear of bleeding, smudging, disappearance.
When the map is complete the page will be completely
Obscured by detail, then a third howl.
Three things about the border are known:
It's real, it doesn't exist, it's on all the black maps.

Geometry Is the Mind of God

A point is that which has no part.
A line is a breadthless length.
A man in his life is a point on a line:
That which has no part on a breadthless length.
The far horizon is a line made of vanishing points,
Near collision of funnelling views,
Flat as a corpse's EKG.
The line to my back
Is a heart attack of granite and ice,
A tumble of similar opposites.
The opposite of a mountain
Is the ocean or the sky
Or an island in the ocean
Or an island in the sky
Or a thorn on the island, growing.
And what regards the reeling firmament
With sympathy?
If the ocean has an island,
If the point has no part,
I'd say it's a green thorn in the heart.

At the Sand Creek Bridge

The path of most insistence
Constrains the creek
Where it spools
And rummages through
Its darkest secrets
And the mooncolored trout revolve.
If it's been a long time coming
It'll be a long time gone.
Or so I think, watching it
Neither hurry nor tarry
Through spills and basins
I used to climb among
With a fly rod between my teeth,
And may again
If life is long.
Now I'm content to idle
The truck on the bridge
As the pines offer
Their shadows to water.
I can still remember
A few things.
The years I wasted fishing
Down here.
Cold rock under fingertips
And the smell of willow early.
The lapidary green
Of the little snake
Who swims like water in water.
The sun getting hotter

On my shoulders,
My feet in the current
Going numb.
Once I stood on the canyon rim
And hurled boulders
One after another down,
To boom and ricochet,
To make the shadows speak.
There was no one anywhere
To hear the canyon's utterance
Or how the quiet rushed back hard
When I stopped,
My loneliness complete,
The smell of gunpowder
In the air.

Druthers

Between permission
and obligation
what light gets in
is sifted fine.
A deep separateness
blesses the evergreens,
ashamed of nothing.
Hardly a day goes by.
The long unlikelihood
suffusing all things
becomes, if left alone,
the same as loneliness.
For instance the kindling
you raked into heaps
by the chopping block,
the rubberbands
you left on doorknobs:
little miracles of sadness,
the order things are in,
a shame.
I never asked
for choices or desire.
I never would have turned.
I'd harvest snow
to live on like the timber does.
Days would go by, restrained.

Left Handed Poem

I am the self of my former shadow.
There's a forest lost in me.
When I walk there the wind scrapes overhead
Like a river I'm at the bottom of.

The opposite of a river,
This furry ridge nonetheless
Flows away and spills itself onto the prairie,
Or maybe it's a root the high peaks need
To fasten them down.

A hundred miles across the sea that went away,
Now windcarved sandstone and cow-specked pasture,
A single peak, triangular
Like a windmill sail,
Lifts itself into the air
And turns the wheel.

Hollow breath of the high couloirs
Turns the branches to water.
Still, but still loud down here among
So much *knowing what to do.*
I can take a hint.
I walk down onto the plain.
Like a small flame I
Steady myself.

What We Said the Light Said

Mystery moves in God-like ways
Is one of many possibilities
And may be why I'm here without you now.

High clouds bruise and white peaks incarnadine.
Slender tree of muliebrity would be another explanation.

Prairie grass, seductive, luxuriates in amber.
Some other
Scraps of clouds the rain left behind
Hunker down for the night in valleys.

The fencepost's shadow leaps out across the plain
Like the bejeezus
Out of someone.

The mirage becomes an oasis
Is something it might have said.
The first stars creep forward
Like wild children coaxed from the woods.

Love, then, was just a sweeter loneliness
Than this,

Though snowbroken aspen across the meadow
Still catch the latest light like a grove
Of saxophones,
Like you said,

Temporary, like eternity,
Though once,
And once again,
Daylight held us on the tip of its tongue
And forgot what it was saying.

It Just So Happens

You fingered the white top
Button of your white blouse.

I just tried to act natural.
A tree fell in the forest

Nearby without making a sound.
Like most of what we said

It made the silence deeper.
Our laughter made us sadder.

You said the only cure
For anxiety was fear.

Now solitude undoes loneliness
Like a ribbon from your hair,

And the sound at last arrives
That knocks the wind out of the ground.

Combat Zone

Peculiarities of temperament
Variously inform interpretations,
Like a siren setting dogs all over town
Diversely howling, or a man walking through
A hair-trigger wheatfield.
Choices concerning deployment of desire
Conform to shapely patterns known as doom.
I don't care who you are.
Whole galaxies of possibility
Smear and dry on the curled floor tiles
Of the peep show booth.
Someone is still alive in the trenches,
Appalled by a stale loneliness,
Dying of meanings,
Enduring for love's say-so.

What wouldn't you do?

Easy Riddle

It's a nail of black water driven deep
And broken off deep in.
It's a lens that stars resolve in,
Like a telescope so strong
It sees through the earth's center, sees stars
On the far side
More imaginable, somehow, than those above,
And the last cigarette
In your delicate and mortal hand
Traverses that heaven
Again and again like a lovesick planet without a hunch
How black the nail, how deep the water,
Holding these reflections up to us.

Holy Saturday, An Exercise in Personification

The jetstream lost its grip and rose
Trailing snowhungry Sonoran air
For a month, like refugees,
But too easy, unbelievable.
Pasque flowers disinterred themselves
Early for the earliest Easter in memory.
For delighters in irony
As the only intelligent, and hence
Predictable, virtue of weather,
The foot of snow,
Expected, followed. The flowers
Close up now, but without terror,
Buried alive again
In a tangible atmosphere of purity.
A prairie of flowers inside a prairie of snow!
They do not ask.
They do not mention the word *forsaken*.
Why should they,
Who have nothing to do but wait and see.

Black Star

No windows in heaven though –
A pat on the back never over.

Was that a gunshot or did someone drop a broom?
Is it the wind or someone sweeping?

Skittish rainclouds glance off the jetstream like seraphic horses
And every day is the provisional ending

So every day the blue spruce float their ridges
To the edge of the sky and wait.

The afterlife will be the same
But without anger. God will be closer

And still too far.

Justice

All around the house huge elms and oaks
Billow up like green thunderheads
In heat that brings cicadas to a boil.
You might think no one's died for a while.
The air is still
Until the tousled willow stirs
From a deeply sexual nap,
And a slight wind
Flips through a paperback
Left open near the open window.
From the way it skims I'd say
This breeze has no interest in the text.
It's looking for some tiny flowers
And four-leaf clovers it would like to have back.
So I take down a notebook I know to be full
Of such flowers and clovers
My mother gathered during her life
Of trying to make the ephemeral last,
And open it near the open window
For the wind to leaf through
And want what it takes.

Sentences for a Friend Snowed In

His snowfences are sentences
Of braille the wind can read,
Though sometimes it ignores his suggestions.

The snowfence is not a fence.

It discontinues,
Contains without surrounding,
Makes the sound of one hand praying.

It holds back the snow by letting it through
And holding back the wind.

Now that Lyle lives alone
His snowfences are fears that say
What he doesn't want to happen.

He doesn't want to be overwhelmed.

He doesn't want to go down,
Snow rising past the windows.

What if the wind indeed prevails?

Spindrift imitates the soul held down,
And the snowfence is a wooden spine that dreams.

The other hand?

Inside – tending the fire.

Synopsis of a Failed Poem

Every simile is elegy,
Resolving in eternal principles.

The axioms are natural, the rules
Are sentimental. Habit animates

The animate, shapely patternings
Accumulate, more awkward to shoulder than trees.

Though not for fear now, images demure.
The lines descend like snowblind mountaineers.

Past
fences the first sheepmen cast across the land, processions
of cringing pitch or cedar posts pulling into the vanishing
point like fretboards carrying barbed melodies, windharp
narratives, songs of *place,* I'm thinking of the long cowboy
ballads Ray taught me the beginnings of and would have taught
me the ends if he could have remembered them.

But remembering
was years ago when Ray swamped for ranches at a dollar a day
and found, and played guitar in a Saturday night band, and now
he is dead and I'm remembering near the end when he just needed
a drink before he could tie his shoes.

We'd stay up all night
playing the beginnings of songs like *Falling Leaf,* about a
girl who died of grief, and *Zebra Dun,* about a horse that
pawed the light out of the moon.

Sometimes Ray would break
through and recall a few more verses before he'd drop a line
or scramble a rhyme or just go blank, and his workfat hands
would drop the chords and fall away in disbelief.

Between
songs he'd pull on the rum or unleash coughing fits that
sounded like nails in a paper bag.

Done, he'd straighten and
say, *My cough's not just right, I need another cigarette,* and

light the Parliament he bit at an upward angle like Roosevelt
and play the start of another song.

Then, played out and
drunk enough to go home, he'd pick up his hat and case and
make it, usually on the second try, through the front gate
and gently list out into the early morning dark, beginning
again some song without end, yodelling his vote under spangles.

Matins

Dawn comes on hard and the peaks take one step back.
Planetary residue eddies in the angling light.
A horse stomps in the yard.
What's it to you?

To apprehend perfection is
To presuppose intention, and we do.
The poem is richer for the writer since
It's my horse.

And it's my neighbor, Frank, in the hospital this time.
Death makes us possessive, I guess.
Its expressiveness depends on imperfection,
Which in turn depends on notions of perfection

Sufficiently out of reach
To prove illusive: *I've known him all my life.*
Roger drives out to bring the cows down for winter
Since Frank is in the hospital.

I see Roger coming ten miles away, pulling horses,
Raising a horsetail of dust at least a mile long
That sizzles down the road
Like a burning fuse.

Grief's Aspect

The cemetery is just a melancholy
Marina and rain
Is the tallest girl I know.

Lookit.
A new slip.
The lawn pulls and swells.

What's amazing is
How manageable it makes us,
As if we were pulling

Over for a siren.
That's why sirens mourn in advance
For what happens.

Special Effects

My shirts on the line
(One sleeve has fondly blown
Around its neighbor's shoulders)
Look like drunks at a funeral.

Raindrops open parachutes
Shading off to snow.

The back fence leans in
And curves down like a breaking wave.

Beyond it
The slender lodgepole pines
Stand so close together
You couldn't walk through them
In your body.

Meteorology

The heart is such a big awkward girl,
I think it's a paper cup of gasoline.
The floor dozes off when I walk across it,
And the windows turn opaque
When they are sure no one is around.

At night when no one sees them
Lovers write each other's names
With black volcanic stones
On the white salt flats.
There were slamming doors and flowers,

A cup of milk left on the stove too long.
There was all the wind in Wyoming.
No one saw anything.
We were not evil enough to make decisions,
But able to let things happen

Evil enough.
We are learning that weather
Is always merciless –
Even if you don't mean weather –
Even the best days.

Materialism

If things aren't things
So much as happenings,
Or a confluence even
More complex,
Then there's no such thing
As sky, though sky
Is real, and we
Have not imagined it.
The everlasting
Never began.
Everything, then,
Is the direction everything
Moves in, seeming
Not to move.
I am waiting
For something very
Nice to happen,
And then it happens:
Your long dark
Hair sweeps
Across my chest
Like sweeps of prairie
Rain. Loveliest
Of motion's possessions,
Hold me still.

Avatar

The imperceptible
Becomes something
Like geese flying,
Or sometimes you hear
A girl's name, that's all.

In many syllogisms
Which begin with words
Like *if morality,*
Narcissism and possibly
Wheelchairs are dignified.

According to a man
Who writes near urinals
In Arcata, California,
The meek don't want it.
And across the street

In another bar,
In the same delirious
Hand and green
Felt-tip pen,
Thelma, do what thou wilt.

Emptiness makes
The world occur more,

Causing love and problems.
The imperceptible
Becomes something

And there you are.

Life Throes

Funny wind,
The grass bends over laughing.
This is a dream you could photograph or die of,
A dream you could nail to a tree.

Because it never ends
I call it *when you leave me*;

Because it never begins
I call it *how I found you*.

I call it *unlike the other small*
When a trout leaps
At a hand-tied fly
Snagged on a low willow branch.

The fish becomes the willow's ornament.
The fisherman is never seen again,

Not in this dream.
Funny wind.

When you leave home, home leaves with you,
Turtle, turtle dove.

It was ever so.
As soon as I look back to see
What's unbelievably
Following still,

As soon as I wave at what I believe in,
It's this dream again,

The one without you.

A limb's sententious crack
Is its apology for breaking.

Far enough is far enough for once.

When we mention *the world,*
We mean our fate before we know it.

I broke as you were mentioning the world.

This is how the moon feels
Whose orbit snaps in apogee.

I wish you wouldn't look at me that way.

My Death as a Girl I Know

I was in a story

In the middle of a field of tall grass
Like someone in a story would
For no reason

It was just as green
It was just as many

When one seedtop brushed another
They both rushed to say
Excuse me quite alright

I smelled music in the piano bench
Gun solvent
A woman's pillow

My sister calls and calls
And I still don't
I like it here when I don't

Let them

Tapping of the wedge and hammer
Father splitting the tree
The tree that split the rock

The rock that spoke
That split in two for the tree

Once

A Safe Place

Because wind is architecture
Independent for its meaning
On any sense of ending,
And light modifies as it asserts,

The hour an angle, a topspin
To get along, on the wire cutters for instance,
The chrome ones I left on your *Essential Horace,*
And because it isn't early anymore mornings

I thought to trace
A windy architecture, circular by nature,
Shot with resolution, because I need a safe place
To keep the wire cutters, here.

And while I'm at it I'm putting in
The angle of your wrist as you draw back from your
Brow that sunstruck auburn hair,
And the way you clear your throat

As if you were about to say something
But then you don't say anything.

Not so much on the land as in the wind,
From where I stand the nearest tree is blue.
The house is log and built to last. It has –
Past the souls who tried to make a life here.
One huge overshoe and a galaxy
Of half moons gouged into linoleum
Where someone's father tipped back in his chair
To formulate plain thoughts and then to speak
In counterpoint to the wind's sad undersong.
He knew the wind was grinding his life away.
Now roof nails bristle obscenely where shingles have flown,
And the blown out panes all breathe astonishment.
The leaning barn is only empty sort of.
It harbors rows of cool and musty stalls. Dark stalls
That haven't held a dreaming horse in years.
I turn to leave, turn back to latch the gate –
Odds on the past to outlast everything –
I walk toward the tree to make it green.

Driving into Laramie

Out here sheer force of sky bearing down
Could crush the town to dust and hand it back.

So it lies low in cringing boxiness
And draws back, as if it didn't know them,
From its own absurdly wide streets,
Which are stupid promises
Where nothing lingers the wind would linger over.

The steeple of the Episcopal church
And the obsolete smokestack at Monolith Portland
Insult the sunshot blue above the levelled town,
The one a washed out dream prosperity woke from,

The other, in this whereabouts, a reflection in the sky
Of the hard thorn in every citizen,
His just belief
That God is impressed above all by defiance.

Death at Work

A Chevy engine hangs by a chain
From a limb of the spreading Ponderosa.

The tool shed smells of stale blood
And is padlocked.

Trying not to be afraid explains everything.

A riding boot slit down both seams
Lolls behind the open door.

The rising sun peeks under cloud cover
As if for purposes of identification
And then disappears for the day.

Hush now,
I promise not to tell any stories
With everyone afraid and trying not to be.

About

Facts about the iris
Do not make the iris
Open. Open your eyes.
It's tomorrow. Call out for someone.

Botany

for RAY WORSTER, 1918–1984, *who died of freezing
on Boulder Ridge, where he was born.*

Shuteye rifted by unspeakables,
All manner of failure to be glad
Returns the inward stare, the tendency...
The tendency of tall notions to fall short,
Small relationships of things to people,
Ray's smokes on the windowsill, for example, to fall
Away and leave their terrible impressions
Here.

The work we do is suffer the above,
As if witness changed what we witness, changed us,
As if the reason we must change were no
More than the rumor of a desert flower
We could not find and so could not betray.

Reading the Will

The violins are doing their laundry.
The world turns on a nail.
This failure has no intention of turning back.
Abstractions like *eschatology*

Consume themselves before becoming.
When accused of theosophy I always maintain
I didn't really mean it,
Even if I mean I didn't really do it.

Imagination is that around which
Mysteries assemble for devotion.
It believes everything, even reason,
Which denies everything. Pay Attention.

My mother willed me her binoculars –
So I still might see her that far away?
Also her silver hairbrush
And other celebrations of anguish.

The durable, once gone, is gone for good.
The ephemeral lasts and lasts.
Abstractions like *eschatology* last and last.
All borders are the signature of fear. Pay Attention.

My mother painted her lips bright red
And held a drop of honey on her tongue.
Hummingbirds kissed her and drank there.
The world turns on a nail.

The Uncertainty Principle

The real is not what happens but what is
About to happen,

Whatever you were dying for before.

Knowing is just feeling
With a sense of direction, and
Thinking tags after like a string of tin cans

Annoying everyone.
Something was about to happen.
Really.

My mother said I'd never make it back
In time by the way she looked at me forever.

She wasn't thinking.

I pledge allegiance to her eyes,
Don't envy me.

When you reach the North Pole the idea of north
Becomes unrealized, free.

Which north was true?
Which south was home?
What is it you are dying for?

Only the stars, which do not know, can tell,
Only the stars, which do not know, can tell.

No

There are no proofs
Only witnesses,
No evidence or guilt,
But crimes ... occurrences ...
Victims, including everyone.
Beyond the conception
Of redemption,
No redemption,
No quivering Jesus.
Roadmaps grow on trees.
What do you want me to be?
Among witnesses, I mean.

Trapper's Cabin

Green fire burning the snow is just the woods in time lapse,
the way God sees them.

           Beavers make mirrors out of freshets,
stob the mountain's bleeders.

             All a beaver wants out of life
is a burglar alarm made from still water, and a sense of *been*
and *going* when he goes.

         Grass chokes down.

                The dead ponds are
living meadows that start to bleed again.

            In the middle of the
meadow a man fashioned a shelter of trees and mud, log ends
axed off sharp, the way the beavers leave them.

             He set his traps
and tried to live awhile, enough.

          Many years after he was done
(I was alive by then) three old ladies, strangers, drove up in
a yellow car, a Hudson, and cleaned the place out – bent chairs,
blue enamel washbasins, medicine bottles blued by sun.

                Then the
roof fell in.

     Then beavers dammed the creek again.

               Imagine the
log shack weathered silver in the middle of the silver pond –
not on an island, mind you, right on the water, floorboards
barely clear.

     Where someone lived and doesn't.

             If beavers had

a king, this would be his castle.

In time lapse, the way God
sees things, it would look like everything – water, grass, house,
water – succeeded out of the ground to be held unharmed in cold,
green flame.

The man whose life awhile this was appears as a
dull aura the cabin has at first, like an electron cloud, that
dully glows and dims.

Post-Modernism

A pin-up of Rita Hayworth was taped
To the bomb that fell on Hiroshima.
The Avant-garde makes me weep with boredom.
Horses *are* wishes, especially dark ones.

That's why twitches and fences.
That's why switches and spurs.
That's why the idiom of betrayal.
They forgive us.

Their windswayed manes and tails,
Their eyes,
Affront the winterscrubbed prairie
With gentleness.

They live in both worlds and forgive us.
I'll give you a hint: the wind in fits and starts.
Like schoolchildren when the teacher walks in,
The aspens jostle for their places

And fall still.
A delirium of ridges breaks in a blue streak:
A confusion of means
Saved from annihilation

By catastrophe.
A horse gallops up to the gate and stops.
The rider dismounts.
Do I know him?

Notes

1. [*page 19*] The title, "Geometry Is the Mind of God," is from Kepler. The first two lines are Euclid's first two "Elements" of Geometry. The heart attack image may have been suggested by a half-remembered line by William Matthews.

2. [*page 36*] The first line of "Matins" was suggested by an image in Bruce Brown's *Mountain in the Clouds*.